Great Leadership

Starts

With

You

Book 1 in the

Covert Leadership Series

Personal Development

By Manny Nowak | Bob Zecca

2nd Edition

DEDICATION

To the ladies that are always there for us, through all we do and all we are. Our life partners who help us to be who we are yesterday, today and tomorrow.

Cheryl Nowak
Robin Zecca

Thank you, ladies, for all you do and all you are.

MANNY@COVERTLEADERSHIPTRAINING.COM
BOB@COVERTLEADERSHIPTRAINING.COM

WWW.COVERTLEADERSHIPTRAINING.COM

Disclaimer

and local governing professional licensing, business practices, advertising, and all other aspects of doing business in the US, Canada, or any other jurisdiction is the sole responsibility of the purchaser or reader. Neither the author nor the publisher assumes any responsibility or liability whatsoever on the behalf of the purchaser or reader of these materials. Any perceived slight of any individual or organization is purely unintentional. I sometimes use affiliate links in the content. This means if you decide to make a purchase, I will get a sales commission. But that doesn't mean my opinion is for sale. Every affiliate link on is to products that I've personally used and found useful. Please do your own research before making any purchase online.

Table of Contents

Introduction

You can have everything in life you want, if you will just help other people get what they want.

Zig Ziglar

Covert Leadership Training

Leadership comes in different styles. We believe:

1. The best leaders are those whose presence goes unnoticed.
2. The next best leaders are those whom people honor and praise.
3. These are followed by those whom people fear.
4. Finally, at the bottom of the scale are those whom people hate.

Where do you and your leadership team fall on this scale?

Remember that when the best leaders' work is done, people say: 'We did it ourselves.'

If you can get your team to this level, you are rocking.

At Covert Leadership, we like to think of leadership in this way:

Managers are the ones who need a map, while leaders use a compass.

We must always remember:

"You are the average of the 5 people you spend the most time with."

So, how are you doing with this?

Who are you listening to?

Who are you hanging out with?

Are these the best people to associate with?

Will they help you become a great leader?

Will those who watch you become great leaders as a result?

To be a great leader, you require discipline.

This is not a USMC recruiting book.

But Manny says, "I can tell you it worked for me, so I want to share the attitude adjustment that happened to me more than anything else. The attitude of success. This is the attitude that Covert Leadership tries to instill in all those who go through our training."

You are amazing.

Just take a look at you!

God built you to be an amazing machine, totally synchronized. Integrated. Built for maximum output.

There is more storage space and processing power in the human brain than in any known computer, despite the fact that the average human brain is much smaller in size than a typical bucket.

Now, what if you take that greatness and transform it into a Covert Leader? You will be unstoppable.

Stop limiting yourself.

> I am the greatest.
>
> I said that even before I knew I was.
>
> Don't' tell me I can't do something.
>
> Don't' tell me it is impossible.
>
> Don't' tell me I'm not the greatest.
>
> I am the double greatest.
>
> Muhammad Ali

We can be our greatest enemy or our greatest supporter when it comes to success.

Once you decide to stop letting things get in your way, you are almost there.

The mental game is a key piece of what makes us successful. Are you ready to become a Covert Leader?

Never put a limit on your dreams, or the dreams of others.

Most of you have watched the Olympics. You've seen those athletes give it their all. They are amazing, aren't they?

But remember, so are you and so is your team.

Most of these athletes have dedicated the majority of their lives, including their childhood, to prepare for winning the gold medal.

They train early in the morning, late at night, during their spare moments, and even when they have no time. They make it happen.

They stick to a schedule. It's the only way they achieve their goals. They are incredibly disciplined and constantly work toward that piece of gold.

Yes, it's all for that gold medal, for the opportunity to be recognized as the best in the world.

That is called dedication. You are dedicated to becoming the best leader possible, and we are here to help you achieve that.

Stretch yourself. Stretch your team.

Now that you have figured out where it is you want to go, I want you to stretch, wherever that is and find out how to go even further.

Many of you might find yourselves in a mindset where you believe you must consistently meet or exceed your goals, leading you to set them at a level you know you'll attain. This is a common practice I often encounter. While it's commendable to exceed your goals, if you have the capacity to achieve 200 units and your goal is currently set at 100, why not consider aiming even higher, perhaps at 250?

Setting achievable goals is undoubtedly satisfying and can boost your confidence, but it often falls short of unlocking your full potential. To truly advance, aim for the seemingly impossible, and you'll find yourself much farther along the path.

Go for Mars, and you might reach the moon. Shoot for the stars, and you may well land on Mars. Dare to set your goals higher.

Remove Your Limits

You can do so much more – but you must remove the limits you have placed on yourself.

If you really want to know what you are capable of achieving, you must be willing to ignore the negative opinions of other people. Those opinions are like rocks around your neck.

There is NO limit to what a person can do or where they can go if they don't mind who gets the credit.

Covert Leadership training is about 3 things:

- Self-Development – YOU!
- Team Development – Your TEAM!
- Coaching Your Team to WIN – To be the BEST!

In this book, the first of three in the Covert Leadership Series, we will address the initial component of Covert Leadership – Self-Development.

Get prepared—and savor the journey.

When you finish this book, we encourage you to consider taking the next step by enrolling both yourself and your team in the full training experience.

The Self Development module consists of four sessions, each four hours in length, delivered once a month. This structure is intentional. It gives you the time between sessions to practice, implement, and apply what you've learned in real-world situations.

Then you return to the next session with questions, insights, and experiences—ready to build on your progress.

This approach dramatically increases retention.

While many training programs result in only about 10% retention, our experience shows this method consistently delivers retention levels well above 50%.

We have also included the first chapter of the second book, "Team Building," for your review at the end.

Let's begin the journey with Bob and Manny and maximize your potential.

Chapter 1

Covert Leadership - 10 Keys of Leadership

I firmly believe that any man's finest hour, the greatest fulfillment of all that he holds dear, is that moment when he has worked his heart out in a good cause and lies exhausted on the field of battle - victorious.

Vince Lombardi

We start by exploring what we believe are the 10 essential keys to help you become an effective Covert Leader. Are there more than 10? Certainly. However, you have to begin somewhere, and that's where our journey starts – guiding you to building yourself into a great leader.

1. **Listen** - Understand your team and understand yourself.

   "Look, coaching is about human interaction and trying to know your players. Any coach would tell you that I am no different." - Bill Parcells

Bob and I have always prioritized building relationships throughout our careers. This approach has enabled us to connect and collaborate with a multitude of individuals, both in our personal growth and within the companies we've been associated with, both in the past and the present.

In sales, it's a common belief that people do business with those they like when everything else is equal. Even when things aren't equal, people still prefer to do business with those they like.

When it comes to leadership, strong relationships are one of your most valuable assets. When you establish great connections with your team members, you can extract much more potential from them than when you don't. This doesn't mean they have to be your friends, which is a separate matter. What it signifies is that you've taken the time to get to know them - who they are, what motivates them, their preferences, and so on. You get the idea.

Covert leadership necessitates that you understand your team members. Start today and allocate a little time every day to learn something about your team.

When a member of your team confides that they're facing challenges at home and shares it with you, it's crucial that the next time you speak with them, you remember to inquire about their situation. These small gestures will lead to remarkable progress.

2. **Energy** - Keeps on going.

    High energy.

    Letting nothing stop you, set the pace.

    You set the example.

The second essential trait of leadership is positive energy– the capacity to go-go-go with healthy vigor and an upbeat attitude through good times and bad. The ability to energize others, releasing their positive energy to take any hill (Jack Welch).

You gave up the option of having off days—days when you're not outwardly enthusiastic and energetic. You have a responsibility, and if you don't feel it, then act as if you do—that's leadership.

Did you enjoy working for a leader who had zero energy and was always looking to leave for the day?

Does it irritate you when you and your partner go to a nice restaurant for dinner and the server is in a lousy mood? Doesn't it ruin the atmosphere and many times the meal? This is part of your responsibility to be cheerful and kind even if you are having an off night.

3.   **Action** - Do something

Action is the catalyst for change; inaction breeds stagnation. How often have you heard leaders discuss their grand plans, their vision for making things happen? Then, six months down the line, nothing has transpired. How does that make you feel? Probably not very motivated, right?

Manny shares, I recall someone, perhaps my wife, telling me, "If you're going to do it, don't just talk about it, take action."

Empty promises and grandiose talk about doing great things while doing nothing leads to negative outcomes. On the other hand, stating your intention to do something small and then actually following through results in significant gains.

4.   **Decision Making** - Make a decision

Manny shares: In my book, "Make a Decision, Will you please," I talk about one of my greatest mentors, Nate. When I was first appointed a manager, as a kicking and screaming computer programmer who just wanted to build software, I could not make a decision.

So what did Nate do? He taught me very simply by never punishing me for making a wrong decision but giving it to me heavy duty when I did not make a decision.

Never vary from the managerial rule that the worst possible thing we could do is to lie dead in the water with a problem.

Instead, solve it, solve it quickly, solve it right or wrong. If you solved it wrong, it would come back and slap you in the face, and then you could turn around and solve it the right way. Or, as Nate would say, if you make a wrong decision, then all you have to do is make another decision to get back on track.

Lying dead in the water and doing nothing is a comfortable alternative because it is without immediate risk, but it is an absolutely fatal way to run a business.

5.   **Expectations** - Always understand them and make sure everyone else does as well.

One of the exercises we do in our training sessions is to teach you how to find out what the expectations of the people you deal with are and share your expectations with them.

When I learned this, it really made another great turn upward in my career. Knowing what is expected can take you to the top; not knowing can get you fired.

How many of us have hired a salesperson and assumed they were on the same page as us, only to learn that they never were? "I thought you were going to sell $100,000 a month." Really, I thought you meant $100,000 a year.

6. **Risk-taking** - As a leader, you have to step out.

This is one of those things that is so hard for new leaders to grasp. How do I take the risk? Can I get someone else to do it?

No, you can't, in fact, there is an old saying Bob and I go by. When we win, the team gets the credit. When we lose, you, as the leader, take the blame. Add that to your pocket of knowledge, and you will be amazed at what you can find.

This doesn't mean making foolish decisions. However, based on our knowledge and experience, we take calculated risks because we believe the potential reward justifies the risk.

Again, we will delve deeper into this concept with some excellent real-life examples during our live class.

Take a moment and reflect on those instances when you chose not to take a risk, even though you knew you should have. How did that decision turn out for you?

Another key point: Many times, it is better to ask for forgiveness than to ask for permission, and usually much faster as well.

Again, speaking of Nate, Bob relates this story about a meeting with him. Bob had asked him if he would give him a warning, an alert when he had crossed the line on risk-taking, so he would know where the boundaries were. A safety net, if you will. Do you know what happened? Nate never issued an alert!

7.   **Single focus** multiple responsibilities - One focus direction.

What is your focus in your company? So many times when we help leaders, we start here. You may be so spread out and scattered that you are doing 10 different things, all going in different directions and wondering why it is not working.

Work with your leaders and focus on one thing at a time. Your team will certainly love it and will be so much more successful. You still have to do many things, but there is no such thing as multi-tasking.

Now your're probably saying that you can multi-task. We'll give you scientific examples to defend our position.

8. **Help** - Your team to be the best. Sometimes, this means leaving them out there to do it themselves.

How do you feel about failure? Of course, none of us likes it but how much have we learned from our failures? Manny relates this experience: You would not be reading this today if I had not learned by failing. It is one of the greatest teachers. I wrote an entire book titled "Failure creates Success".

Remember the story Manny told of Nate, our mentor? He never gave me a hard time about the wrong decision, only about not making one.

So when you work with your team, you have to give them the room to learn, to make mistakes, and to grow. We do correct them and help them learn, but if you do everything for them, their growth will be very limited.

9. **Integrity** - Never compromise it.

Manny relates this story: Someone once told me integrity is your greatest asset as a leader. It is your core and the barometer of how your team knows who you really are. There is a great book titled "The Speed of Trust "by Stephen M. R. Covey, all about trust. Your integrity makes you a great leader or a poor one.

10. **Perseverance** – Never...Never give up.

Bob relates: You don't practice until you get it right... You practice until you can't get it wrong.

I love this saying. It can really change the way you look at things. Many of us have been taught to practice until we get it right, and we have been doing that. Not that it is a bad thing, but that is just the start of the race. Once you get it right, how can you make sure you do not get it wrong? Amazing results will follow you with this mindset.

We are off on the Covert Leadership trail. Thanks for coming with us, and much success to you.

Chapter 2

Knowing Your People is Key to the Success or Failure of an Organization

Give me six hours to chop down a tree and I will spend the first four sharpening the axe.

Abraham Lincoln

Now let's take a deep dive into the people you need to ensure your organization operates at an optimal level, creating a fantastic workplace that's both productive and profitable. How do you implement the right leadership to achieve this?

Leadership Starts with Your Strengths

Have you ever done a SWOT analysis, recently or in the past?

Strengths.

Weaknesses.

Opportunities.

Threats.

If not, take a moment right now, look in the mirror and ask yourself these four questions.

1.   What am I really good at?

        What are my strengths?

        List the things you feel define your greatest abilities.

2.   What are my greatest weaknesses?

        What do I really struggle with and what drives me crazy?

        List the things you feel define your greatest weaknesses.

3.   What are the greatest opportunities that sit in front of you
        today?

        What should you jump on?

        Again, make the list.

4.   What are the greatest threats before me today?

        What could really throw off my game?

        What could derail our plans to move us forward?

One thing we stress at the Covert Leadership Seminars is to focus on building up your strengths. I learned many years ago that if you focus on what you are already good at, you will not just become better, but you will become one of the best.

Manny relates this story: When I was a young man, I was a real mathematics brain. Fast and quick, math was just so easy for me. Instead of being challenged, I got bored. When you get bored with one of your strengths, it can be dangerous. So, I encourage you to work on your strengths. As a leader, I encourage you to work on the strengths of your team.

The second thing we focus on is opportunities. Each day, numerous opportunities pass us by, often unnoticed. It's essential to learn how to recognize and be receptive to them. However, to be effective, we also must know which opportunities to pursue and which ones to let go. This distinction can make all the difference.

Keep your SWOT analysis; we will be coming back to it later in the program.

Do you inspire others to do better, to be more successful in their areas of strength?

Manny relates: Someone recently told me a great story about motivation versus inspiration. You see they believed that motivation is external; you can only do so much from the outside. However, Inspiration, is what we have inside us, and once you release that, there is no telling how far you can go.

This is what we want you to remember as we go through the Covert

Leadership process. Let it get inside of you, inspire you, and make you the best leader you can be.

True leadership lies in guiding others to success.
      Ensuring that everyone is performing at their best.
      Doing the work that they are pledged to do.
      Doing it well ~ Bill Owens, American Photographer

What will happen to your team if you help guide them to success? If you placed them in the right areas and helped them perform at their best. Will that make a difference to your organization? When people are positioned where they perform best, the entire company benefits, and your organization can achieve amazing results.

When you return to your organization, take some time and find out the strengths of your players, encourage them, and then help them move forward.

As you will learn in this training:

- Management is doing things right.
- Leadership is doing the right things ~ Peter Drucker, Author

You need managers and people who are doing things right by making sure others are doing things right. You are with us because you want to do more. You want to do the right things. You desire to become a

Covert Leader.

Managers look inward.

Leaders look outward.

Remember that effective leaders encourage contrary opinions, an important source of vitality. Are you doing that?

Are you seeing it in your organization?

If not, you could be missing out on some of the best answers for the future.

Always remember that Leaders are obligated to provide and maintain momentum as well as be responsible for effectiveness. A ship going in the wrong direction is not getting any closer to the desired destination, no matter how fast it goes.

Some qualities of great leaders include:

Compassion

Sincerity

Passion

Sensitivity

Honesty

Confidence

Positivity

Courage

Determination

Integrity

And the one we believe is most important in great leaders –
Humbleness.

You may never think of yourself as a leader until slowly you become one.

When you look behind you, is anyone following you?

You will be amazed at how many great leaders are humble, and when they look behind themselves, they are amazed by the number of people who are following them.

Leadership is at its best when:

- The vision is strategic.
- The voice is persuasive.
- The results are tangible.

Our organization needs a strong leader, not a dictator.

We like to believe that leadership requires these four pieces:

- Select for talent.
- Define the right outcomes.
- Focus on strengths.
- Find the right fit.

To succeed, you must either discover the talent that can lead you to your defined destination or commit to developing that talent yourself.

Next, you must define the right outcomes for your organization. Not your best outcome, not the world's best outcome, but the best outcome for the company you are leading.

We told you in the beginning we would be focused on strengths.

First, you identify the strength, and then you must find the right fit for that strength.

As it was stated so many years ago in the great book by Jim Collins, "Good to Great."

First who...then what:

- Get the right people on the bus.
- The wrong people off the bus.
- The right people in the right seats.
- Then, figure out where to drive.

These 4 points are one of the keys to Covert Leadership. You have to asked yourself these questions when you look at your team and organization.

Do I have the right people to take the organization to the next level?

If you have some of the wrong people, you must be willing to make changes.

Once you have the right people, you have to find the right place to put them in.

Then you can figure out where to drive to.

You are not a leader to win a popularity contest.

You are a leader to lead.

Don't run for office—You're already elected.

If you want to be in politics, then go for it. In business, you have to lead, and you don't necessarily have to be popular. So many people are afraid of what other people think. That is not leadership.

In the end, you still have to do what is right, not what is popular.

Someone once said there is less stress in bad news than in uncertainty.

Think about it.

People want certainty. Even if it is bad news, they will handle it better if it is certain.

Remember, being the leader doesn't guarantee that what you say will automatically happen.

I believe this is one of the earliest lessons we learn as leaders. You say, "Go left," and then wonder why everyone's heading to the right?

Leaders must ensure that their organization possesses a straightforward, comprehensible, and clear plan for the future.

Strong leaders are decisive. They don't allow mediocre efforts to persist and potentially drag down the organization.

Learning to make decisions, implement change, and ensure it works is essential. The fear of this is prevalent in many organizations today. If you want to be a genuine leader, start by eliminating the marginal efforts of your team today.

You have to regularly close down the low & medium efforts.

That takes <u>courage</u>.

It takes being different.

It takes leadership.

Expending too much energy trying to motivate people is mostly a waste of time and energy. You have the wrong people. We'll cover this in team building. It is better to spend that energy to help people become inspired. Remember what we said initially "inspiration over motivation," but inspiration comes from inside. Inspiration is fueled by encouragement, and it may even be fueled by motivation in some cases.

The idea is not to stimulate passion but discover what makes you passionate. Do you know what makes you passionate? But even more, as a leader, do you know what makes your team passionate?

Vision – Shows an end state where all the plans and strategies will take you.

Manny relates this story: I have been working with one leader for the past 6 years. Many times, I am about to end the relationship, but this individual possesses such a profound vision that I can't bring myself to do it. It really is true that visionary leaders move us forward. It is also true that visionary leaders are many times hard to lead.

Tactical – Shows how to achieve the vision by executing. This is a real issue in today's organizations. They are not getting it done; they are not executing very well. They are not able to pull the trigger to make the decisions.

Manny shares this story: I was recently working with an organization and asked this question in my research, "Does your management do what they say they are going to do?" I learned very quickly that "management always talks about what they are going to do, but they never do anything." Don't be that person or organization. If you say you're going do it then do it regardless of the outcome. Remember failure creates success.

Plan – Specific step-by-step process on how to implement a strategy. Make sure you have one.

Budget – Financial piece of the plan. Remember that without the money, nothing happens.

The single biggest way to impact an organization is to focus on leadership development.

There is almost no limit to the potential of an organization that recruits good people, raises them up as leaders and continually develops them. ~ John Maxwell, Author

Becoming a leader is synonymous with becoming yourself. It is precisely that simple and it is also that difficult. ~ Warren Bennis, Author

Three Important Requirements for Leading Others according to Robert Katz?

He identifies these skills that are essential for a successful management process:

Technical skills – you must know how to do it.

Conceptual skills – you must be able to see it.

Human or interpersonal management skills -and, of course, you must have people skills.

As both Bob and Manny will tell you, this is really number one. Our success is based on the ability to build relationships that get things done.

No matter where you go in leadership, the following two may hit you. They can always be there to greet you.

1.   You don't have a clue what this business's problems are all about.   Wait until you have to turn around a failing business and cannot find the issues you need to fix.

2.   You are so connected to the people that you don't have the emotional resolve to get rid of people you have affection for and cannot do the job.

       Now I realize I have to constantly cut before it becomes an issue, not wait until after it becomes a problem.

We all want to have smooth sailing, but as the captain, you look out on the sea and realize you have zero control of the weather. Think about that as it relates to people.

You have to sail the ship, so what do you do to be successful?

Let's conclude this chapter with a few simple points:

Hire people with passion:

- Inspire them.
- Give them aggressive goals & incentives.
- But also tell them what behaviors will get them fired.

And never forget, growth for growth's sake is sometimes detrimental to the business. We'll share personal experiences along these lines in the live seminars.

Chapter 3

Self-Development – Delegation

And be not conformed to this world: but be ye transformed by the renewing of your mind, that ye may prove what is that good, and acceptable, and perfect, will of God.   Romans 12:2

In this chapter, we will look at these four areas as they relate to delegation.

Why can't people Delegate?

Our Eight Ingredients of Delegation.

Why is Delegation so difficult?

What you can delegate and what you shouldn't.

The function of leadership is to produce more leaders, not more followers. ~ Ralph Nader

Before you are a leader, success is all about growing yourself. When you become a leader, success is all about growing others. ~ Jack Welch, General Electric

Think about it – the above quote is by the man who made this a science, Jack Welch. He created more high-level leaders from GE than any other CEO, more than 35. He knew it was not about how many followers he had but rather about how many leaders he built, all with their own followers. Our mentor Nate created many leaders, including Bob and I.

Again, the question is, how many great leaders have you created?

To create great leaders, you have to learn to delegate.

This chapter is all about delegation.

Delegation is a key ingredient in leadership, yet why is it that so many people can't get it right? I wrote a book about it because I kept hearing so many complaints, "Why are you trying to do it all? You have a team; why not have them do some of it."

Bob relates this story: I had a VP came to me and complained that he had the work of 10 people. My response was, "That's why you have 10 people on your team".

When you become a leader, you change places. No longer are you judged, rated, promoted or for that matter, anything else you personally do. Instead, it all now comes down to what you can get done through others.

So many one-time leaders have stopped and gone back to being a non-leader. They would rather do it themselves than get it done through others. Nothing wrong with that, but don't give up so easily.

The better you are at what you do, the harder it is to get someone else to do it. They never seem to be able to do it as well as you. Thus, you just end up doing it yourself.

But that is the "Wrong answer."

The question I challenge you with is, "Why is Delegation so Difficult?"

Take a moment and think about it. Then give me four reasons you feel that way.

Write them down.

1.

2.

3.

4.

Take a few moments and really think about the reasons you came up with. Spend some time talking about this with other leaders both inside and outside your organization. This is a lively discussion during our training classes, and if you get to come, please bring your reasons and what you learned with you.

Now, let us take a deep dive into this question and see what we come up with.

So, why can't people delegate?

1.   When you delegate a task, you give up the responsibility for its execution. But you are still ultimately accountable for the success or failure of the task.

Someone else has to make it happen when you are so use to doing it yourself.

Someone else has to do it, and if they mess up, you are the one who is going to get the blame for it being wrong.

You have to allow people to make mistakes in order for them to learn. Yes, in some fields, it is not easy because the cost is too high, so you have to keep those tasks for now. It is, however, the routine daily stuff that people have a hard time allowing someone else to do and make a mistake doing it.

Key point to remember: Do not say: "I have done that a thousand times; what is the matter with you."

2. Environments where managers lack confidence and trust in their subordinates therefore find it difficult to delegate work to them.

Here we are again, back at the trust issue.

But trust is just the start; you also now have the confidence issue coming into play.

Do you trust your players?

If not, why not?

If not, what are you going to do about it?

"Nothing" is never the right answer.

You have to find a way to trust them, or you have to replace them. It really is that simple.

You must have trust to lead.

Yet, many leaders cannot get through this point.

Trust is the foundation of confidence. To help your team develop their own confidence, you must trust them with the responsibilities you delegate their way. As they gain confidence they'll also begin to place trust in you. Once trust is established delegation becomes significantly easier and more successful.

Yes, we all cringe when we have to delegate work to certain players on our team. Again, we are back to the issue. You have to learn, or you have to make some changes.

3.   Unwillingness to let others make mistakes and carry the blame.

How many times have we said, "oh forget it, I will just do it myself."

Wrong answer.

Not just the wrong answer but totally the wrong direction. You will never learn to delegate if you don't let them do it. Let them make a mistake. Let them learn, grow and develop. Mistakes are part of the learning process. Fear of mistakes can hold people back from developing.

4.   Time. You tell yourself there is never enough of it to explain and show the task that has to be completed.

Then make the time. In the long run, you will save much more than you gave.

Understand that you have to make time now because if you do, then in the future, this person will have to be able to do it themselves and do it well.

Being in IT we always heard the phrase when developing code 'Never time to do it right, always time to do it over'. Take the time now.

You will struggle and most likely fail to become a great leader doing all the work.

You must work with your team to make it happen. You must delegate the work, and they have to do the work.

Manny shares this story:

One afternoon, I was sitting at my desk, working on ideas. I was the president of a technology company and called in my three lieutenants. Something came up, and I delegated it to one of them. He fired back at me, *"Manny, we are always wondering, what do you do? You seem to give everything to one of us."* I simply looked at him and said, *"Correct."*

You know you have learned delegation when you get to that point.

5.   Control.

You are relinquishing something that you normally do and maybe staking your reputation on that person therefore, it is best that you do it yourself. The problem is, how many of these can you do yourself before you get overloaded or before you start getting sloppy? Delegation is being in control of what gets done, not in doing it.

6.   I can do it better than they can.

Well, of course, you can do it better. At least in most cases.
What you learn after a while is that the other person, the one
who could not do it that well to start with, actually is now doing
it better than you ever did. And that is a plus. That is the goal.
When your team does the things you used to do better than you
ever did, you have taken a major leadership step forward.

7.   Credit for doing it.

You might get credit early in the cycle, but after a while, your
boss will start looking at what your team gets done and not at
what you do.

This is where so many leaders get into trouble. They don't
delegate, and sooner or later, they just plain get overwhelmed
with way too much to do.

Yes, the person you give the task to might fail. OK. Then we go
back, teach a bit and make them get up and do it again.
Learning from our failures and mistakes makes us so much
stronger. We have the wrong ideas about mistakes. Mistakes
are tools that help us to learn and to get even better. When are
we going to start understanding that?

Thomas Edison once said '"I have not failed. I've just found
10,000 ways that won't work."

8.   Fear that someone else might do the task more effectively.

        They sure might and confident leaders hope that they do. When
        that happens is the time you will begin to shine. I need you to
        start understanding wholeheartedly that what your players get
        done actually reflects on you. It can make you look bad, or it can
        make you look great.

9.   The leader may be insecure and fear becoming redundant if
        they delegate.

        Most of this comes from a lack of understanding. Remember
        that leaders get credit for what they and their team,
        department, division, company, and so forth get done.

**Delegation self-assessment – please go to this link and do the
Delegation Self-Assessment.**

https://www.linkedin.com/pulse/self-assessment-12-questions-
determine-how-well-you-delegate-roberts/

This is a great piece that will help you understand yourself better.
Also note the 5 levels of delegation that are at the end of the
survey.

How did you do?

In the training, we spend a lot of time understanding the results.

Eight Ingredients of Delegation

- Directions – what-how-who-what-if.
  You have to give the people you assign a task some direction.
  They do not know what you know and will not know it for a
  while. So tell them more than you think you need to. As they
  learn and grow, you'll find yourself needing to provide them
  with less and less guidance. Eventually, they'll understand
  what's required and start taking initiative on their own. Look at
  the five levels of leadership in the survey you just took.

- Rationale – why?
  Why do you want me to do this? The answer is not, "because I
  said so." My mom used to pull that one all the time. Tell them
  why it makes them even more effective and decreases the
  learning curve. But be careful, you do not have to explain
  everything every time. They will learn that when you ask them
  to do something, they know it is important, you need it done,
  and you trust them to do it.

- Outcomes – expectation.
  You need to understand this one very well. What do you expect
  the person to do, and what results do you expect that person to
  bring back to you? Further, define what they should expect
  from you to make it happen. When both parties know each
  other's expectations, you will be amazed at the results you get.
  Expectations are key to better leadership and greater success.

- Authority – decision making.
  Get this one very clear in your mind. When you give responsibility, you also have to give the authority they need to get the job done. Without the authority, it's just not going to happen and it will cause a bunch of frustration.

- Deadline – when is this due?
  When do you want it? When they understand the expectations, they know the what; now they need to know the when. Just one point of clarity: make sure they understand when you want it. It has some but not necessarily an exact relationship to when it is due. A better direction is, I need this by [specific date or time].

- Feedback – do you understand what I just gave you?
  Do you have any questions? Do you know what you need to do? Do you have the authority you need to make it happen?

  All this being equal, there is no reason it will not get done.

  Make sure they understand that they need to come back and ask if anything is unclear as they work through the process.

- Follow-up – progress review.
  For longer tasks, keep checking. Where are they in the cycle? Do they need help? What questions do they have? Set up a schedule for regular reviews on longer tasks and projects. The key I learned when I was a project manager at Boeing was the importance of conducting weekly project reviews. Sometimes it may only take 5 minutes but always make sure they are on point.

- Support – your availability.
  Be there to help make them successful. I want you to do this. I will give you all the guidance you need, but you are responsible for doing it.

What Can You Delegate

Okay, you now know you can delegate. The next question for you is, what?

What can you delegate?

- Routine stuff that you do every day. As you rise in an organization, it is more important for you to start giving everything away that someone else can do. Back to my story earlier.
- Interesting tasks that will make them think.
- Task others could do better than you.
- Tasks that others might find enjoyable, but you prefer to handle yourself.
- Tasks good for the development of your team. Meaningful stuff that will help them grow.
- Whole tasks, give it all to them, not just little crumbs.
- Time-consuming tasks that you just do not have time to get done.

Delegate anything that someone else is capable of doing so that you can focus on the tasks that only you can accomplish, at least for the time being. Got it?

What Can't You Delegate

- Ill-defined tasks that you do not understand.
- Confidential Matters – that you cannot share.
- Crisis situations that you need to handle as the leader.
- Praise or reprimand. Giving credit is fun; reprimanding is not. Neither of these can someone else do for you.
- Planning the development of your team. This is all you.
- Tasks for which you are personally responsible.

Before you Delegate – You Need to Know these points.

- Their skills – or this is a great way to find out
- Areas in which they need improvement.
- Tasks they like and dislike. You can work both ways with this one.
- Their personal development goals. Knowing your players is critical to success.
- The resistance they may put up and the best way you can handle it.
- Their current and future workloads

Are you ready to delegate everything you can?

We cannot over-emphasize the criticalness and the importance of this process. Both Bob and Manny have been successful because they do this very well. But even more, they have been able to develop great leaders who often go out and become even more successful than they are.

Chapter 4

Decision Making

"The number one characteristic of a good leader is the ability to make things happen."
— John Maxwell

To quote Manny, "When it comes to leadership, this is one of my favorite areas today."

But that wasn't always the case.

In fact, early in my career, I struggled with decision-making. I hesitated. I overthought. I second-guessed myself. And if it wasn't for a great mentor who pushed me, I may never have developed this critical skill.

Today, I teach leaders something very simple:

You learn decision-making by making decisions.
And many times, that means making the wrong ones.

Because when you make a bad decision, you're forced to make another decision to fix it.
That's where growth happens.

The Reality of Leadership Decisions

Outstanding leaders make decisions:

- **Effectively**

- **Quickly**

- **With confidence**

Let us ask you a question:

How many times have you hesitated when you knew you needed to decide?

And more importantly...

What did that hesitation cost your team?

As you rise in leadership, something very important happens:

- You have **less information**

- You have **less time**

- The **impact is greater**

So if you struggle making small decisions that affect one or two people...

How are you going to handle decisions that impact hundreds?

The Hard Decisions Leaders Must Make

Let's make this real.

The financial reports come in.
Six months—bad numbers.

Now the company has to make cuts.

And not small ones.

Two hundred people may need to be laid off.

Can you make that decision?

Because that's leadership.

Not the easy days.
Not the wins.
Not the celebrations.

Leadership shows up when the decision is hard.

7 Principles of Powerful Decision Making

1. You must move forward without all the information

If you're waiting for perfect information...

You'll be waiting forever.

Great leaders make decisions with **incomplete data** and adjust as needed.

2. You must handle the pushback

No matter what decision you make...

Someone won't like it.

Sometimes a few people.
Sometimes a lot of people.

That's part of the job.

3. You may be unpopular in the short term

Study great leaders long enough and you'll find something in common:

They all went through seasons where they weren't popular.

But they stayed committed to the **right decision**, not the **popular one**.

4. You must have conviction

You cannot hide behind:

"Well, that's what corporate wants..."

That's not leadership.

Leadership is ownership.

Even if you don't fully agree...
Even if it's uncomfortable...

You stand behind the decision and move forward.

5. Time will force your hand

Sometimes you don't get time to think.

Sometimes the answer is needed...

Right now.

And the question becomes:

Are you going to step up...
Or step back?

6. You must handle the impact

Some decisions affect people's lives.

Jobs.
Families.
Careers.

That weight is real.

And yes—you may lose sleep over it.

But leadership is not about avoiding impact.

It's about carrying it responsibly.

7. You will make the wrong decision

Let's be clear:

You will get it wrong.

Both Bob and Manny have. Many times.

The question is not:
"Will you fail?"

The question is:

"Will you learn?"

Because if you learn...

You don't repeat the mistake.

And that's how leaders grow.

Manny Shares a Lesson From His Mentor

One of my greatest mentors taught me something I've never forgotten.

He never punished me for making a bad decision.

But if I hesitated...
If I didn't make a decision...

He was all over me.

Why?

Because the worst thing a leader can do is nothing.

Remember This

It is easier to ask for forgiveness than for permission.

Now, that doesn't mean being reckless.

It means being willing to act.

Because momentum matters.

Critical Thinking: How Leaders Decide

As a leader, you are constantly:

- Identifying opportunities

- Choosing between options

- Advising others

And here's something important:

If you're struggling between two choices...

It usually means they are very close in value.

So what do you do?

You decide.

Developing Other Leaders

When you are coaching your team:

Don't just tell them what to do.

Instead:

- Walk them through the options

- Explain the outcomes

- Help them think

Then let them decide.

Because a **recommendation** is the seed of a decision.

And your job is to grow decision-makers.

Decision-Making Under Pressure

Let's test you.

Case 1: Payroll Problem

Payroll is due in 3 days.

You need $50,000.
You have $32,000.

What do you do?

Case 2: System Failure

New system launches Monday.

It's Sunday at 4 PM.

Major issues still exist.

What's your move?

These are not theoretical.

These are real leadership moments.

And in those moments...

You don't get to wait.

Final Thought

Let us leave you with this:

Make a decision... will you please.

Because in leadership—

- Action beats hesitation

- Progress beats perfection

- And movement beats standing still

Every single time.

Chapter 5

Self Development - Selective Attention

"If you don't like how things are, change it! You're not a tree." Jim Rohn

Definition: The capacity for, or process of, reacting to certain stimuli selectively when several occur simultaneously.

Wow, that is a mouthful.

But what does it really mean?

It simply means this – the ability to select the right path when many paths are laid out before you at the same time.

For example:

Four of your employees are pushing you in four different directions; which one do you deal with first, and how do you handle the rest of them?

You need to allocate funds and the deadline for some of the deals is today. How do you decide to push for more time or let the funds fall through?

You have 3 meetings today, 5 phone calls to make, 50 emails to read, 2 projects to review and approve or decline, and this is just what's on the schedule!

This is part of all our daily work as a leader in the organizations of today.

Now let's take a look at what is being said out there about Selective Attention:

The process of directing our awareness to relevant stimuli while ignoring irrelevant stimuli in the environment.

This is an important process as there is a limit to how much information can be processed at a given time.

Selective attention allows us to tune out insignificant details and focus on what is really important.

Just think of what you could do in your job day in and day out with this ability at its peak performance. Think of how you could be an even more effective leader dealing with the situations that arise each day.

Selective Attention Example

Many of your top individual sports athletes do a phenomenal job of "being in the zone" and blocking out every distraction, concentrating on one thing and one thing only.

A couple of hours into the day, I realized I hadn't really been paying attention to anything. I knew there was something playing in the background, but I couldn't hear it. My focus was entirely on the report I needed to produce, and the rest of the world seemed distant and vague.

This is an example of selective attention.

Selective Attention is when the conscious awareness is focused or controlled on something, and you tune the rest of the world out.

Selective Attention

Can be very useful when used in the right situations. Let's look at some of these.

1. Filter things out so you can focus on the task at hand. How can you get anything accomplished when there are so many things going on at once? You need to focus your attention on one thing.

2. Noise – it is very hard to eliminate the noise in most situations today. You, as a leader, cannot run around with earbuds in your ears tuning the whole world out. If only it was that easy.

3. Distractions -then, of course, there are these.

   The Phone – interesting how many people just can't put it on silent. How many people just can't let it ring or send it to voice mail. You, as the leader, have to set the example for the rest of the team.

4. Email – We always have to ask in each seminar, how much time do you spend on email every day? Now, some of it is very productive, but so much of it is just eating up your time. The average leader today can spend anywhere from 2-4 hours in email. I read once that Bill Gates only read his email once a day from 2-3pm. Can you do that?

5. Text – over the past 6 months, you may have already noticed exponential growth in this area of your business and personal life. I can't get you via email, so what is your cell phone number so I can text you when I need you. Guilty as charged. I tell people all the time this is how to get to me.

6. Drop-ins – I often wonder how some people get anything done in their office. Someone is always dropping in to chat. If I shut my door, which used to work, they just knock and say, "Hey, I see your door is closed. Do you have a minute?" ***No! Why do you think my door was closed?***

Selective Attention more:

What happens when your team has selective attention and you are not one of the top priorities on their listen list.

What happens when you have selective attention? Wow! How does it make your team feel to think you are not listening to them? Trust me, it sucks. If this is an issue for you, I highly suggest you get into the course we do on Covert Leadership. We deal with this very well through role-playing. Having selective attention can really kill an organization's future growth.

What happens when your supervisor has it? Again Wow! When a client is not listening to you, it is easy – it is your money. But when your boss is not listening, that spells trouble. I need you to listen. I need your help. You set the stage.

What do you do if you can't experience selective attention? You need to get some help. Here are some additional resources for you to look at.

Selective attention definition, ideas, tests.

https://www.mentalup.co/blog/selective-attention

Video and quiz and course.

https://study.com/learn/lesson/selective-attention-theory-examples.html

18 Selective Attention Examples

https://helpfulprofessor.com/selective-attention-examples/

Chapter 6

Self-Development

Emotional Intelligence

"A coach is someone who tells you what you don't want to hear, who has you see what you don't want to see, so you can be who you have always known you could be."
Tom Landry

Emotional Intelligence - The capacity to be aware of, control, and express one's emotions and to handle interpersonal relationships judiciously and empathetically.

"Emotional intelligence is the key to both personal and professional success." Especially to becoming a great "Covert Leader."

Six benefits of emotional intelligence.

1.   Increased Leadership Ability – When you are using your emotional intelligence, you have much better skills to correctly deal with the people you supervise. You see an employee come in with a totally different expression on their face than you see every day. If you are on your game, you note to yourself that this is an issue. You become aware, and that is the first critical step.

2.   Increase team performance – You can increase your team's performance by huge numbers. Understanding the feelings of your players takes you to a whole different level in dealing with them day by day.

3.   Improve Decision Making – as we have discussed, "Can you make a decision." Or, as I say in the book, "Make a decision, will you please." Emotional intelligence can help you greatly in this area.

4.   Decrease occupational stress – have you been in my shop lately – the stress level has gone over the top.

5.   Reduce staff turnover – Keeping the right people is a tremendous asset to so many companies throughout the world. When we have the right players in the right seats, they have a greater tendency to stay. Yet, they can still decide they are going to leave.

Some people are very good at hiding the fact they are going to leave; those are the ones you need to find and understand for 2 reasons.

      A.   They have important information you need to know that you might not know. Things that are going on in your organization and your leadership that you are blind to.

      B.   You do not want to lose a powerful resource just because of a situation you would have handled were you aware of it.

6.   Increase personal well-being – When the team is rocking, so is the leader, and vice versa. When people are happy and doing what they love or doing what they don't love with the right attitude, it takes your organization to a whole new level.

What makes up Emotional Intelligence?

Think of emotional intelligence as a circle in the middle of the page. Then, think of 4 circles around it, each touching a piece of the main circle. Each of the surrounding 4 circles has one of these points in it.

1.   Personal emotions – Knowing your emotions in situations as well as your team's emotions in those situations. How many of you can do this successfully? Do you know your team?

2.   Understanding emotions – Once you work with people regularly, you become aware of who they are and what they care about. You begin to establish a successful relationship with them. The process to understand them has begun. How many times has your frustration stopped you from dealing correctly with people because you just don't understand them?

How come this person gets so emotional? It is strange.

How come they just don't listen? Are they thick or what?

Why can't they make the goal? What is the matter with them?

Sometimes, it is all about the emotions, so take some time to understand them. Then you will understand better what you need to make it work.

3.   Handling emotions – Understanding them is key but handling them correctly is even more important. You have to be able to handle the emotions as a leader. What to do and what not to do. Today, it is harder than ever before. Add HR and Legal to the equation and you could get yourself in real trouble.

4.   Using emotions – Finally, how can you use your emotions and your team's emotions to move the organization forward and become even more productive?

This is never meant to be used in a negative way but rather to help both you and the person you are trying to lead.

Emotional Intelligence.

Let's take a look at the five components.

1.   Self-awareness – how well do you know yourself? How much time do you spend trying to understand who you are and how you operate? As a leader, how much time do you spend on your team and trying to understand these same areas?

2.   Self-regulation – are you self-regulated? Does your boss, friend, or even your spouse do it for you? Keeping you under control? What is it with you, what is it with your team and what is it with each of the players on your team?

      Manny shares this story:I have a great friend who is totally self-motivated beyond belief. It's great, but as a leader, he has a real issue because he thinks everyone successful is just like him. If they are not that way, he has no time for them. That is the wrong answer!

3.   Motivation – what motivates you? Motivation is an external stimulus. What do you need to read, see, understand, feel, or touch? What external stimulus motivates you? Same with your team. The key takeaway is this: if I know what motivates my team, I can at least take a step forward in moving the players. What motivates you, your team, and your team players? If you want to be a "Covert Leader," then you need to know and understand these triggers.

4. Empathy – do you know what it means? We all know sympathy means feeling bad about something or with someone, but empathy is a much more powerful tool. Empathy means you have experienced the issue that they are going through yourself, and you can personally relate. Do you know how much more important and how much closer you can get when you have been there yourself? I always like to try and find someone on my team to help someone else who has already gone through the same thing.

5. Social Skills – I hear a lot of chatter these days about social skills today. I hear about how some generations hitting the workforce just don't have these capabilities at all.

   I'm not sure I agree with this, but I do agree that without these skills, your leadership is much less powerful. Plus, if you have a team with these abilities, they will be totally unstoppable. If they can interact with other people socially, they are way ahead of the group.

   As I heard in a sermon not long ago from a 30-year-old preacher, don't give up on this new generation. They will get it. There is so much for the good of us all in the generation; keep working with them.

Emotional Intelligence

Here are some examples of what emotional intelligence in the workplace looks like:

1. People express themselves openly and respectfully without the fear of offending co-workers. Sometimes, we call this a very soft environment. People are not afraid to tell the truth because they know no one is going to jump down their throats if they do. Yet, there are so many environments where this is not the case. As a leader, you must understand that you need to create an environment where people can express themselves without fear.

2. Resilience is evident when new initiatives are introduced. The team takes them, turns them into the best results, and makes it happen.

3. Flexibility is present – but I must caution you on this one. Flexibility is key, but it can also get out of control very easily, resulting in an even bigger problem. We gave tremendous flexibility during the pandemic, but now many organizations are having a hard time going back to how it was before.

    Did we take flexibility, or were we forced to take it to a dangerous level? I have to tell you this is a major concern we are looking at with so many of our clients today.

4.   Employees spend time together outside of work. When you get here, you know you have created a very successful team. They enjoy spending time together but be cautious because this can potentially lead to additional challenges for you as a leader. What happens when a player enjoys spending time more with the team than with their spouse or children? It does happen. You, as the leader, have to deal with this correctly and successfully.

We've only scratched the surface in this area. There is so much more here that can help you.

For more on this subject, please Google any of the subject lines below:

Emotional Intelligence and Leadership

How to Improve Emotional Intelligence at Work

Emotional Intelligence 2.0, by Travis Bradberry and Jean Greaves

Chapter 7

Self-Awareness

The most terrifying words in the English language are:
I'm from the government and I'm here to help. Ronald
Reagan

Self-awareness is conscious knowledge of one's own character, feelings, motives, and desires.

Be cautious of the fact that "the process can be painful, but it leads to greater self-awareness."

When you know your character and who you are: when you know your feelings and how to deal with them, your motives and your desires, it makes you a much better person.

Knowing your team player's character and who they are, their feelings and how to deal with them, and their motives and desires makes you a much better, stronger leader and allows you to get so much more done for your organization.

Self-Awareness

We like to think of "awareness" as what you notice in life. *It's about paying attention to what is going on.*

If "awareness" is about noticing stuff in the world, "self-awareness" is about focusing your awareness on yourself.

How aware are you of yourself, what you do, and how you do it?

If you have self-awareness, would it make a difference in your life as a leader? Would it make a difference to your organization and to the success of your players and your organization?

Self-awareness – how to practice it and make it part of you.

The first step for practicing self-awareness is gaining a greater awareness of your emotions. This is an area we tend to hesitate on for ourselves.

How much time and effort have you spent trying to understand your emotions?

Manny shares: I used to be a very emotional child; tears would come to my eyes, and it was hard to deal with. However, when you become aware of your emotions, it sets you on the path to managing them and using them for success. Emotionally sensitive individuals can lead effectively, but learning to express and control their emotions is crucial to their success.

As we keep saying, knowing your emotions and becoming self-aware is where you start. Knowing the same about your players can lead you to build a great team that creates amazing success for the organization.

The second step to practicing self-awareness is making a habit of tracking your feelings. Chart it, write it down, track it. It is important for you to know when these emotions come into play in your work life.

This is a great way for you to help your team deal with their emotions. Have them write them down and then work with them to understand and overcome the negative effects they can have on the players.

The third step for practicing self-awareness is expanding your practice to areas of your life beyond your feelings. Feelings are good when used in the right ways. Now, how do you expand beyond the feelings?

Self-awareness plan to move forward.

1. Seek Feedback – feedback is the key to determining how this emotion of yours affects your team. It is important to know how it affects your boss, your clients, and those you work with. When dealing with your team, ask them to do this. It will be amazing what they can learn.

2. Self-Reflection – think about it yourself, reflect on what happens and why. Again, you, as the leader, need to learn this about your team.

3. Be aware of others – how they operate and how you would behave reporting to them. Understand this while you are near them or working with them. It is why you work very well with some and not so well with others.

4. Using assessments for understanding yourself and your team. In our session, we work with self-assessment tools to help you to understand yourself better.

Assessments are a great way for your team to learn more about themselves and for you to learn more about them. In fact, many companies use these tools today to actually hire personnel.

Manny shares his first experience with them as a manager, and how to this day, he still uses those skills in his career:

It was a management retreat for the managers and their spouses, and everyone took the assessment. It was called TDF (and still is). I learned a great deal about how I made decisions, but even more, I learned how my wife made decisions and why we were off balance so many times. I learned that I was more of a feelings-type person while she was more of a thinking person. If I gave her time to think about it, then it worked so much better. Even today, I still know I'm what they call a small "T," which means thinking was low on my scale and high on my wife's. Therefore, if I let her do the thinking and I use feelings, then together we can make a sound decision – Wow!

But even more than that, think of the effect on your team if you do an assessment like this together. Yes, there is some hesitation, but work through it; the results are amazing.

Check out: www.TDFInternational.Net

Thank you for being part of the Covert Leadership process. This book provides a brief overview of what is covered in detail in our seminars, where interactive exercises and peer feedback really bring these concepts to life.

Information is useful because it prompts new thinking.

Practicing implementing the information you learn by attending a seminar creates tangible muscle memory that dramatically increases your ability to implement these concepts.

Your leadership is determined by how effective you are at implementing these Covert Leadership best practices. Practice with us by scheduling your seminar at:

www.Covertleadershiptraining.com

Or Call us at:

856 364 5867

Thanks Bob and Manny

Preview of the next book of our 3 part series

Chapter 1

Team Building

"Leadership is not about titles, positions, or flowcharts. It is about one life influencing another." - John C. Maxwell

Team building is all about taking the strengths of all your players and creating a team that will excel so far beyond the norm that it will build your organization into a super company.

The end product is a powerful team. So much that the team runs itself, and eventually so does the company.

You, as an individual, have only so many strengths.

Most of us have about 3 and only one is a superpower.

Now just imagine a team of 9 people, each one with a superpower different from all the others. Wow! What could the future look like with that combo?

So many times when building a company or a team, we look for people like us. That is not always the right answer. Yes, from certain aspects, they should share our values and integrity, but they don't necessarily need to have the same strengths as us.

Look at a baseball team. If you have two players, both super catchers who can hit, field, and work the pitcher, great. But what do I do with the second one? Does he/she just sit on the bench? Yes, having a backup is great, but it doesn't work that way in business. It is important to have the right players, but each player has to have unique skills that will help the team move forward.

Having the right powers in your organization is critical; using them effectively and stretching them to new levels is even more important and is your job as the leader.

Let's look at your team's strengths.

Take a moment and highlight the top 5 strengths of your team.

Then ask yourself, What am I missing?

Do I have duplication?

How can I take advantage of these strengths to grow my organization?

The Answers to these questions will help you see what you need. Now, it is up to you and the team to go out and make it happen.

Let us take a deeper look at team building.

First, don't fall into the trap of assuming the hierarchal boss must always be the team leader.

In real life, as most of you know, there are many times when it is an informal leader who is really calling the shots.

Manny shares this experience: Recently, I had the chance to work with an organization that was having some issues making their teams work the way they needed. Productivity was way behind in meeting the organization's goals. I listened and asked a great deal of questions. What I found was that the real leader was the informal leader. The formal leader was not doing anything to help the team with the task at hand.

This, as it turns out, was an easy fix. I simply made the informal leader the formal leader and moved the current formal leader to another position in the organization, more adaptive to his skill set.

It is not always that easy. Many times, the formal leader puts up a huge fight. Many times, the informal leader is good where they are but not necessarily in the formal leadership position.

So, you may have to be more creative to make it work. Give some power to the informal leader.

Split the position into two positions. Terminate the formal leader.

Manny shares this story: I recently had a situation where the formal leader just would not give anything meaningful to the informal leader. It was causing a real problem within the organization, and things were not getting done. It was becoming a battle. The solution we came up with was simple. We split the job into two pieces, with each player responsible for their piece as we broke them out, and both now reporting to the boss.

A key to success in a team is that the goals should not solely mirror the leader's beliefs or convictions.

To be truly effective, the goals must incorporate the team members' views and desires as well.

This is called listening, and if I have not stated it yet, it is one of the two most important skills you can have as a leader: the ability to listen. The second skill of being a great leader which we will get to later is you must be humble. But let's get back to the story.

When it comes to setting goals for the team, the team must be involved.

I know you want the team to follow what you want and that you get your direction from your boss. Still hand-me-down goals will not work. There is no conviction. Hand-me-down goals are those that you just come in with and try to get the team to follow. They are your goals, and you are simply pushing them on the team where they have zero input.

Take your goals, discuss, and work on them. Then, as a team, come up with those that you can make happen.

Manny shares this story: In my days leading sales teams, I always took the corporate goals and worked them with the team. We usually went higher than the company forecast on sales, but the team built them and was committed to their success. The number was owned by the team, not by the company and not by me alone. The difference is that they had the opportunity to contribute their input to these figures. Trust me, this is a critical success factor to make you a great Covert Leader.

You might be asking the question, "What if they had come up with goals short of the corporate ones."

Two possibilities:

A.   I would continue to work with the team until their goals got a bit higher.

B.   I might have to go back to the corporate decision-makers and let them know their number is unrealistic and too high.

This did happen, and it is important that you remember that if your team feels it can't be done and you can't convince them, the goal may be wrong. Don't hesitate to trust your team. Don't hesitate to go back and battle if necessary. Remember you shouldn't make every goal you set. If you do they most likely were too low. Yes you'll have the rare occasion where you do and if so congratulations however it usually is an anomaly.

Deeper dive into Team Building

Groups become teams through a number of actions. Let's walk through some of these together.

1. Disciplined action – knowing what they need to do and having the discipline to get it done. The team should always know what they need to do. They should always know where the team stands on the process and always have the self-discipline to make it work.

2. The team shapes a common purpose – This is our purpose as a team. It can be a very simple purpose statement you as a team put together. Write it down and work it as a team. I know you may think this is not accomplishing a great deal, but when it is always right there, and each member can refer to it, it really does make a difference.

3. Agree on performance goals.

    This really relates to expectations. What do you expect from your team and what do they expect from you. Lay it out clear as day and you will have fewer issues. I have found that when we are all on the same page with expectations, the rest is so much easier.

4.   Define a common work approach.

How do we work as a team so that we all are successful? Is it Jim's way, Mary's way, or Tom's? I simply say we are going to do it the right way regardless of whose approach we go with. It may not always be easy for everyone, but remember, we are a team, and a team needs to operate the right way, not as you may want it to. As long as you can justify we are doing it the right way, there really is no issue.

5.   Develop high levels of complementary skills.

We need to work as a team. What I do needs to complement what you do, not go in a totally different direction. As a Covert leader, you must make sure this is happening in your organization. If it is not, then you must take the action needed to make it happen.

Do not replicate the path that so many organizations take and ignore it, hoping it goes away; it doesn't. Bite the bullet and do what needs to be done.

Hit it head-on.

Don't leave elephants in the room.

Deal with the issues that prevent the team members from doing it together.

A great team does one thing very well. They hold themselves mutually accountable for results. I am not just accountable for my stuff, but also to a degree of what each member of the entire team is responsible for as well. The same goes for every member of the team. If you can make this happen, the team will achieve amazing results.

A practical example might be a great firefighter team. Each member has a specific responsibility that affects every team member to achieve a specific outcome. In this case, saving lives and putting out the fire. If one member fails, it could be catastrophic for the entire team. Everyone knows their responsibility and everyone else as well.

6.   A good team must demand candor and objectivity from each other.

Does your team have the freedom to be candor and objective? Not just with each other but with you, as the team leader as well? If your players can have candor with each other and not with you, it will result in creating things that are hidden, which occurs in many organizations. This often results in problems being passed up to top management and dealt with there, which can lead to uncomfortable decisions.

Why do you think so many organizations cannot deal with what is going on? They just don't know how to be candor, nor are they able to be objective. We'll cover this in another chapter on Assertiveness. They have to do what other people expect. Dump that thinking. Success means, let's throw it on the table and see what we learn. Let's work it, let's be honest, and let's talk about it truthfully.

Some of the best teams I have had the privilege to work with understand this. I am working with a team right now that understands this and that is why we have created such great success and triple-digit growth.

7. Strong personal commitments to one another's growth and success distinguish high-performance teams from weaker teams. Do your players care about each other and the success of the other players on their team? I recently worked with a team that demonstrated this fact to an amazing level. When one of the players was failing or falling behind, the entire team did what they needed to do to help that person be successful, learn, grow, and, next time, be able to help others on the team. The player went from being a weak link to one of the strongest in selling. It is a commitment that few can make today. It takes an all-out effort, but in a tight organization where people really care, this again is a propelling factor that makes a Covert leader different from the rest.

8. Great management teams debate vigorously in search of the best answers yet unify behind decisions regardless of parochial interests. I've been in situations with a room full of Type A personalities, each believing they are right and have the best solution. It can get almost out of control. Yet what comes to the table, what comes out, is the stuff super companies are made of. When someone looks in from the outside, they might think these people do not like each other, but the truth is they are simply trying to get all the pieces on the table so the best solution can be found. Remember, much gets accomplished if you don't mind who gets the credit.

Once done, they come out with the best answer, and even though it might not be what I wanted, I have given my input, and it has been considered. Now, this is the decision we came up with, and I, and the entire team is 100 percent behind it.

Manny relates this: One of my clients and I routinely go through what we call cat and dog fits like the above. Yet when we are done, we are on the same page, and we go out to lunch.

You can't always have it your way, but as long as your way gets on the table and is discussed and considered, you are going to be alright. If the team makes the decision, you, as a member, have to support it. That is how strong teams operate.

Also, remember that your job as a Covert Leader is to put together and then try to formulate a high-performance team. You may look like the dumbest person on that team, but remember your goal as the leader!

Also, as a Covert leader, being too involved and interfering too often is a de-motivator. You set the goals, and everyone knows what to do. Unless there is a problem or decision that only you can make, stand down and let the team do what they do best.

More From Manny and Bob:

Please give us a review on Amazon, we really appreciate it.

Thank You.

What makes great leadership training

Great leadership training is more than just teaching participants a set of skills. It is about helping them to develop the knowledge, skills, and attitudes that they need to be effective leaders in their specific roles and organizations.

Here are some of the key elements of great leadership training:

- Focus on whole-person growth. Covert Leadership training is divided into 3 pieces, Development of you the leader, development of your team, and finally, teaching your team to win consistently. Leadership is not just about having the right skills and knowledge. It is also about being self-aware, resilient, and able to build relationships. Great leadership training will help participants to develop all of these areas.

- Be interactive and engaging. People learn best by doing. Great leadership training will provide participants with opportunities to practice new skills and get feedback from others. Covert Leadership makes effective use of role playing and mastermind to carry this out.

- Be supported by coaching and mentoring. Leadership training is just the beginning. Participants need ongoing support to implement what they have learned and to develop as leaders. Coaching and mentoring can provide this support both internal and external.

Here are some additional things to look for in a great leadership training program:

- Experienced and qualified facilitators. The facilitators should have a deep understanding and experience in leadership and be able to deliver the training in a way that is engaging and effective.

- A variety of learning methods. The training should use a variety of learning methods, such as lectures, discussions, case studies, guest speakers and simulations. This will help to ensure that all participants learn effectively.

- Opportunities for feedback. Participants should have opportunities to get feedback on their progress throughout the training program. This will help them to identify their strengths and areas for improvement. This is accomplished in Covert Leadership training by the interactive format of all we do.

- A focus on application. The training should focus on helping participants to apply what they have learned to their own roles and organizations. This will help them to become more effective leaders. Thus Covert Leadership Training is made of 3 two day segments with at least 2 months between each piece. This allow you the leader to apply, get feedback and adjust what you learn in a real live environment.

If you are looking for great leadership training, be sure to consider these factors. By choosing a program that is relevant, tailored, interactive, and supported, you can help your employees to develop the skills and knowledge they need to be successful leaders.

Contact us:

Manny@CovertLeadershipTraining.com

Bob@CovertLeadershipTraining.com

Website:

www.CovertLeadershipTraining.com

Linkedin Page:

CovertLeadershipTraining

A Leadership Seminar from two former CEO's

COVERT LEADERSHIP TRAINING

Module 1: Self Development

Module 2: Team Development

Module 3: Coaching

Leadership Skills

Team Building

Assessment

Delegation

Execution

Decision Making

Selective Attention

Assertiveness

Winning Consistently

Emotional Intelligence

Conflict

Plus each day includes one or more of these activities:

Master Mind Round Tables

Mock Boardroom Meetings

Ice Breaker Exercises

Team Projects

Book Presentations

Guest Speakers

Assertiveness Workshops

Role Playing Sessions

Speech Giving Practice

Full Series…..3 Modules 6 Full Days…Two consecutive days every other month

OR

Take the first Module (Self Development) and then decide to continue with the rest of the series.

www.covertleadershiptraining.com

95% of the material presented in this Leadership seminar has been experienced in leading companies by our CEO's

Still Not Sure Covert Leadership Training is for you – Read on:

Principle One

Covert Leadership helps your leaders to become the most loved leaders in the organization.

Question:

Are your leaders loved by their followers?

Do they generate top level productivity?

Do they produce excellent Results?

Do their followers give it all?

Think about this:

Great leaders are not necessarily the most liked, but they are the most loved.

Look at the great leaders you have worked for or that you have observed.

Everyone did not necessarily like them, but so many loved them.

Loved leaders are the ones who can make decisions, get things done through other people, are trusted, honest and hardworking, results driven people. When all is done, those who work for them believe they did it themselves.

Principle Two

Covert Leadership helps your leaders get more done through other people.

How many times have we taken a star performer, made them a leader, and watched them fail? Not because they could not do the job, but because the skills they needed to lead, are not the skills they needed to be a star performer. The attitude is right, but the skills are not.

The greatest villain in our story is leaders unable to get things done through other people at the same super level they use to do it themselves.

This external issue causes your leaders to have an

Inability to

Make decisions.

Effectively delegate work.

Teach how to do it with patience and empathy.

Coach their team to consistently win.

This leads to internal issue of

Frustration

Anger

Lack of the level of success they are used to having.,

What your leaders need is to experience the same success in leadership that they have experienced in the rest of their lives.

What your organization needs is leaders who can do this.

Principle Three

Covert Leadership is your guide, we help you to be the hero.

We know your frustration, we empathize with your dilemma, we care that your team becomes the best leaders.

Bob and Manny are leaders, they have lead, they are still leading, but even more they are helping to develop you into leaders better than they ever could be.

You leaders will be the best.

This is not text book, academic learning.

This is real life stuff.

This is stuff your team can relate to, can identify with and can learn from

This is the stuff that makes your leaders the best.

Principle Four

Covert Leadership has a plan, a process and direction.

Three keys in Three Sessions.

1.   Self-development – Developing the leader

                        Leadership Skills

                        Delegation

                        Selective Attention

                        Emotional Intelligence

Decision Making

Perseverance

Assessment

2.   Team development – Developing the leaders' team

Disciplined action

Shaping a common purpose

Assessment usage

Agree on performance goals.

Define a common work approach.

Develop high levels of complementary skills.

Hold themselves mutually accountable for results.

High Performance Teams

Context switching

Assertiveness

Resolving conflicts

3.   Winning the game – creating successful results through your team

Coaching and Mentoring

Mastermind Session

Assessment usage

Pressured decision making

Winning consistently

Team Projects

Assertiveness workshop

Our Training Format:

All training occurs at a location remote to your office.

There are assignments required before the first session and in between sessions.

All meals, beverages, and materials needed are provided. Ample breaks are scheduled through-out the session.

Principle Five

Covert Leadership takes you and your team to the extreme.

What happens when you don't take your leaders to their limits?

People who don't get the opportunity to become great leaders, go someplace else where they can or go back to being a producer. Many of the best people are lost this way.

What happens when you make people leaders and don't spend time and money making them the best.

What is the cost of not doing this program to your organization.

Principle Six

Covert Leadership creates the leaders that will help you take your organization to the next level and way beyond that.

1.   Winning power and position.

    Leaders who know how to get things done through others.

    They grow the organization, and they grow themselves.

    They are your tomorrow.

    There is an extreme shortage of great leaders out there.

    But you can develop your own with Covert Leadership Training.

    You can have the leaders that win consistently.

    You can develop a team of Covert Leaders.

2.   Victory for your organization

    Growth

    Profit

    Success

    The frustrated leader is replaced by the great leader.

3.   Inspiration

    Your leaders can become the next Jack Welch or Steve Jobs

    Acceptance.

Their teams give 100% consistently.

They love their leaders.

www.CovertLeadershipTraining.com **856 364 5867**

www.ingramcontent.com/pod-product-compliance
Lightning Source LLC
Chambersburg PA
CBHW032028290526
45786CB00011B/1089